GUIDE
TO
RAPID
REVISION

SECOND EDITION

Daniel D. Pearlman
Paula R. Pearlman

ODYSSEY
A Division of

Bobbs-Merrill Educational Publishing
Indianapolis

The Bobbs-Merrill Company, Inc.
4300 West 62nd Street
Indianapolis, Indiana 46268

Second Edition
Fifth Printing—1977

Library of Congress Cataloging in Publication Data
Pearlman, Daniel D.
Guide to rapid revision.
1. English language—Idioms, corrections, errors.
2. English language—Rhetoric.   I. Pearlman,
Paula R., joint author.   II. Title.
PE1460.P37 1974   808'.042   73-20076
ISBN 0–672–63300–0

GUIDE TO RAPID REVISION

PREFACE TO THE SECOND EDITION

We offer the Second Edition of this *Guide* in the hope that it will achieve the ends of accurate and rapid revision even more effectively than in the past. The chief changes in this new edition are of the following kinds: 1) refinements and expansions of material in already existing sections; 2) the addition of new entries, namely, *Brackets, Clichés, Hyphens,* and *Unity of Sentence Parts;* and 3) the streamlining of the overall format to make this *Guide* a greater time-saver than ever.

We owe thanks to the many teachers and students who have used our *Guide* over nearly a decade and offered suggestions for its improvement. In this new edition we have incorporated every positive criticism offered except those which would have necessitated major changes in the book's scope and function.

A NOTE TO THE TEACHER

We have long felt that the process of revision, central in the development of writing skills, has not been accorded the full attention it merits among books published for courses in English composition. The composition handbooks are designed primarily for *class* study of the problems of writing in a sequential and topically organized manner. The student who turns to them, depending on their aid when revising a paper marginally annotated by his teacher, finds that he loses time hunting for the passages relevant to his particular problem, and that he often must read as much as a full chapter for each error he has committed.

The present *Guide,* planned entirely with the realities of revision in mind, provides the student with *immediate* answers to the specific problems he encounters, gives him sufficient information to solve them, and yet does so with *brevity*. Using the book independently, the student may feel as if the teacher were personally going over his paper with him point by point in conference.

Among the major time-saving features of this *Guide* are its compactness and the alphabetical arrangement of its contents. Another convenience is its Table of Correction Symbols, which in this new edition doubles as a Table of Contents. The Table represents a gathering of the most common symbols used by English teachers throughout the country, and at the end of the Table there is space for students to list extra symbols that professors may use from time to time. A student referring to the Table can revise his paper with no uncertainty as to his teacher's system of notation. We call attention also to the realistic examples, culled from actual student papers, that illustrate the various types of writing deficiencies. In the brief explanations which in most cases follow each example, the general rule for revision is concretely applied.

Since the *Guide* is designed for independent use by the student, it becomes feasible for the teacher to have his students spend a class period now and then revising their papers under his direct supervision. The clear, compact treatment of each topic in this *Guide* will enable the student to overcome a considerable number of his weaknesses in short order; and the demands levied upon the teacher for individual help will be reduced to a workable minimum. You may find, also, that if each student is required to maintain the *Progress Charts* included at the end of this *Guide,* you will be able to diagnose at a glance, during conferences, the student's overall writing problems.

The *Guide to Rapid Revision* has been found valuable both in courses where a regular handbook of composition is assigned and in those, also, where no handbook is used. The *Guide* substitutes for the larger handbooks insofar as it contains an adequate treatment, in spite of its small physical compass, of the basics of English style, usage, and mechanics.

A NOTE TO THE STUDENT

This book is designed to save you many hours in revising your compositions. Our aim has been to make explanations brief, clear, and to the point, and to include realistic examples that you can apply to correcting any specific shortcoming of your own. Years of teaching experience have convinced us that most of your writing problems can be eliminated in short order. To attain our aim of brevity, however, we have sacrificed no information that could cast real light on your writing difficulties. At the same time that you work at each revision, you learn the principles of English usage, so that you need not fall into the same wasteful patterns next time around.

How to use this Guide: If your instructor uses correction symbols, and you are not certain of their meaning, the alphabetically arranged Table of Correction Symbols found at the beginning of this book will tell you what the symbols mean and what page to turn to for help. This book avoids lengthy grammatical explanations of your writing problems. Specific examples combined with short, concrete explanations show you how to overcome your weak points.

Special spelling problems are handled in the sections on ABBREVIATIONS and NUMBERS, and in the GLOSSARY OF COMMON ERRORS IN DICTION (see DICTION). We take it for granted that in the usual case of a misspelled word you will refer to your dictionary. If, in addition, you keep up to date your general *Progress Chart* and your *Spelling Progress Chart*—included at the end of the *Guide*—you will have an excellent understanding of your writing problems and what to bear down on as the term progresses.

All in all, we trust you will find this *Guide* the remedy you need against the headaches of revision.

D. D. P.
P. R. P.

CORRECTION SYMBOLS

GUIDE TO RAPID REVISION

ab ABBREVIATIONS

As a general rule, do not use abbreviations in your writing. **Spell the word in full.**

Some of the most common ink-saving habits to get rid of are the following abbreviations: *&, gov't., U.S.* or *U.S.A.* USE: **and, government, United States, United States of America.**

A common "thought-saver" to avoid is *etc.,* short for *et cetera,* meaning *and so forth.* If the reader is not acquainted with everything you might mean by *etc.,* you can not expect him to read your mind and fill in the exact items you are thinking of.

Exceptions: With proper names, always use the abbreviated titles **Dr., Mr., Messrs., Ms., Mrs., Mmes., Jr., Sr.,** and **St.** (Saint).

Other standard abbreviations are **A.M., P.M., A.D., B.C.,** and those of certain well-known organizations and government agencies, such as **FBI, NATO, NASA.**

abst ABSTRACT EXPRESSIONS

Be more specific: **1. Add a word or phrase to the abstract term** to define it more carefully. **2. Replace the abstract term by a word or explanatory passage** that expresses your meaning as concretely as possible.

ABSTRACT TERMS:

Abstract words and phrases, like *beauty, evil, progress, the American way,* have meanings that are somewhat different for every individual reader. Perhaps you are certain of what you mean by "progress" in a statement such as this: "America has made great progress in the last fifty years." But your reader does not know what you mean until you use a more *specific* expression such as "technological progress" or "moral progress."

To avoid vagueness, you would no doubt further have to explain an expression like "moral progress." Do you mean that the divorce rate has gone down? Do you mean that teen-agers are more "moral"?

The effect of further explaining yourself is to get more and more *specific* and *concrete* in the ideas you project. The more precisely you define your ideas, the smaller is the danger of your being misunderstood.

CONCRETE TERMS:

A word is truly *concrete* when it refers to an actual object whose nature people are generally agreed on. For example, we all know what *tree* stands for. However, when the tree you are writing about has a place of importance in your composition, it is better to use an even more specific concrete expression, like *elm, oak,* or whatever it might be. It is like zooming in for a close-up in movie-making.

Example:

Abstract: *Politics* unfairly determined the results of the recent election. (Many of us, in attempting to explain the ills of society, take the intellectually lazy way out by shrugging our shoulders and blaming everything on *politics,* a word used vaguely to cover all sorts of shady dealings by people in high places.)

Revision: *A last-minute public smear campaign together with private blackmail* unfairly determined the results of the recent election. (It turns out that the abstract "politics" was screening some rather interesting *concrete* realities.)

adj

ADJECTIVE

Change the marked word to an adjective.

Poor: The American *education* system is undergoing radical changes.

Better: The American *educational* system is undergoing radical changes.

Certain verbs, like *look, sound, smell, taste,* and *feel,* are usually followed by adjectives instead of adverbs. (Adjectives used in this way describe, or "modify," the subject and are called predicate adjectives.)

Examples:

He looked *good.* (Use *well* only if you mean that the person no longer looks *ill!*)
The food tasted *delicious.*
She feels *good.* (She feels *well* means she is no longer *ill.*)
The music sounded *wonderful.*
The flowers smell *fragrant.*

adv ADVERB

Change the adjective to an adverb (usually by adding -*ly*).

In careless or very informal kinds of speech one hears errors such as the following, which unfortunately creep into one's writing:

Poor: She sang *beautiful*.
Better: She sang beautifully.

Poor: He writes *good*.
Better: He writes well.

Poor: They had a *real* good time.
Better: Avoid expressions such as *real good, real nice,* and use instead *rather good* or *very good*. They had a very good time.

agr AGREEMENT

1. Make your verb agree in number with its subject. If your verb is in the singular, change it to the plural, and vice-versa.
2. Make your pronoun agree in number with its antecedent (the word your pronoun refers to).

1. SUBJECT-VERB AGREEMENT.

In ordinary sentences you can easily see how the subjects and verbs agree in number, as in the following examples:

He speaks well. (Singular subject, "he"; singular verb, "speaks.")

They speak well. (Plural subject and plural verb.)

Carol, Iris, and John *speak* well. (Subjects connected by "and" take the plural verb.)

Your mistakes occur in sentences where you are not sure of what the true subject is, and where you do not know whether the subject is singular or plural.

a. Don't be fooled by words and phrases which come between your subject and verb. Find the *simple* subject (the subject stripped of all its modifying words and phrases). *The simple subject is never part of a prepositional phrase.* But prepositional phrases often follow your subject and confuse you, as in the following sentences:

Poor: The solution to all our problems *are* staring us in the face.

Better: *is.* (The subject is *solution,* not *problems,* because "to all our problems" is a prepositional phrase.) **The solution to all our problems is staring us in the face.**

Poor: One of the requirements of membership *are* monthly dues payments. (Notice that two prepositional phrases, *of the requirements* and *of membership,* come between the subject *one* and the verb.)

Better: *is.* One of the requirements of membership is monthly dues payments.

b. In some cases, normal sentence order is reversed and the subject *follows* the verb.

Poor: After the cheerleaders *come* the band.

Better: *comes.* (The band *comes.*) **After the cheerleaders comes the band.**

Poor: There *is* two dogs in the park.

Better: *are.* **There are two dogs in the park.** (Be careful of sentences beginning with *there* followed by a verb. *There* is never the subject—except in this very sentence! The subject will always follow the verb. In this example, *two dogs* is a plural subject, and therefore takes a plural verb. But note this important exception: "There is a bottle of wine in the cupboard and a thick hunk of cheese." Although *bottle* and *hunk* form a double, or compound, subject, and should logically take a plural verb, *are,* we keep the more natural sounding *is.* The *idiom* of the language sometimes violates grammatical *logic.* As long as the *first part* of the compound subject in a "there is" sentence is singular, the verb may also remain in the singular: "There *is* one man against the proposal and five men in favor of it."

c. When singular subjects are joined by *either-or, neither-nor,* use a singular verb.

Poor: Neither the captain nor the coach *have* much experience.
Better: *has.* **Neither the captain nor the coach has much experience.**

If one of the subjects joined by *or* or *nor* is plural, then the verb agrees with the nearer subject.

Poor: Neither the captain nor the coaches *has* much experience.
Better: *have.* (The plural, *coaches,* is nearer to the verb.) **Neither the captain nor the coaches have much experience.**

Poor: Neither the coaches nor the captain *have* much experience.
Better: *has.* (The singular, *captain,* is nearer to the verb.) **Neither the coaches nor the captain has much experience.**

2. PRONOUN-ANTECEDENT AGREEMENT.

Example: *Bill* knows *he* is smart.

The pronoun *he* refers to *Bill. Bill* is the "antecedent," the word referred to by the pronoun *he.*

Example: Immediately after buying his *books,* he lost *them.*

The antecedent of *them* is *books.* Notice that in both these examples, the pronoun agrees in number with its antecedent: *he* is singular, as is *Bill; them* is plural, as is *books.*

You make most of your mistakes when you forget to use a singular pronoun to refer to words such as *each, one, every, everybody, everyone, anybody, anyone, nobody, no one, either, neither.*

Poor: Everybody raised *their* hand.
Better: *his.* **Everybody raised his hand.**

Poor: We felt that each of the workers loved *their* job.
Better: *his.* (The antecedent is *each,* not *workers.*) **Each of the workers loved his job.**

amb AMBIGUITY

Ambiguity means *double* meaning or else *vagueness* of meaning. **Revise the ambiguous passage to make it clearly mean one thing only.**

Ambiguous: As soon as she entered the room, she was *struck* by the handsome stranger.
Clear: As soon as she entered the room, she *found the stranger strikingly* handsome.

Ambiguous: Bob asked Jack if Iris liked *him*.
Clear: Use direct quotation. If *him* stands for Jack, write: "Does Iris like you?" Bob asked Jack.

(See REFERENCE OF PRONOUN and MISPLACED MODIFIER for further examples. If the ambiguity is a general *vagueness* of meaning, see ABSTRACT EXPRESSIONS.)

ap, apos APOSTROPHE '

Add a missing apostrophe, or remove one you have mistakenly used.

The apostrophe has three main uses: 1. It marks the possessive case of nouns. 2. It indicates a contraction. 3. It is used in plurals of letters, abbreviations, and numbers.

1. FORMING THE POSSESSIVE CASE OF NOUNS:

a. For nouns, both singular and plural, that do not end in *s,* form the possessive by adding ['s]: the *bird's* nest; the *children's* party; the *person's* name.

b. For plural nouns that end in *s,* add the apostrophe only: the *soldiers'* uniforms (uniforms of the soldiers); *ladies'* coats (coats for ladies).

c. For singular nouns that end in *s,* add [*'s*]. But if the last *s* would be awkward to pronounce, then drop it and add only the apostrophe: the *boss's* daughter (daughter of the boss), but *Rameses'* kingdom, *Moses'* leadership.

d. Do *not* use an apostrophe to spell the personal pronouns *his, hers, ours, theirs, whose.*

2. THE APOSTROPHE IN CONTRACTIONS:

Always use the apostrophe to show the omission of a letter or letters in the contracted form of words: *wasn't* (was not), *I've* (I have), *we'll* (we will), *you're* (you are), *it's* (it is). NOTE: As a general rule, avoid contractions in formal writing.

3. PLURALS OF LETTERS, ABBREVIATIONS, AND NUMBERS:

a. Lowercase letters: *n*'s, *x*'s, *p*'s and *q*'s. (But for capital letters, either *Q*s or *Q*'s.)

b. Abbreviations using periods: B.A.'s, C.P.A.'s, R.N.'s. (But for abbreviations without periods, either VIPs or VIP's.)

c. Numbers: *either* 5's, 10's, the 1900's, *or* 5s, 10s, the 1900s.

AWKWARDNESS

The word, phrase, or passage marked is awkward and should be entirely rewritten.

The cause of awkward writing is often sheer haste. The writer does not allow his phrasing to mature in his mind until it fits in grammatically and stylistically with what he has just been writing. Frequently, a confusion of competing phrases results, as in the following example:

"As long as a man is enjoying what he is doing, *where his environment is,* and whom he associates with, he is happy."

The writer did not want to sacrifice the fancy-sounding word "environment" for the simpler, but stylistically preferable, *where he is.* The resulting awkwardness is simply verbal and does not obscure the thought. In the following example, however, hasty choice of a verb ("thriving") to cover a three-part subject ("money, success, and education") turns the thought itself into a logical absurdity:

"Our present world is quite materialistic; it is a world in which *money, success, and education are thriving* over the love of nature itself."

For one thing, does it make sense to say that money is "thriving"? Secondly, why does the idealistic writer include a normally positive goal like "education" among goals like "money" and "success," which he evidently scorns? Indeed, this sentence is so awkward that a complete revision might have to run like this:

"In our present materialistic world, our love for nature can not thrive in the face of our greater craving for money, success, and the kind of 'education' that helps us attain these goals." (See also COHERENCE.)

[ ] BRACKETS

Use brackets to surround editorial insertions in a quoted text and to avoid parentheses within parentheses.

"Every village, every town [in Spain] is the centre of an intense social and political life," says Brenan.

Kafka's most extraordinary work begins with the description of a man suddenly changed into a giant beetle (*The Metamorphosis* [Original German edition: Leipzig, 1915]).

cap CAPITALIZATION

Capitalize the word or words indicated, or else make them begin with a small letter if you have incorrectly used capitals.

1. Capitalize proper names. These are the names of specific persons, places, things, races, institutions, organizations: **Joe Fox,** the **East River, Negro, Tilden High School,** the **United Nations.** (Note: the word *the* beginning names of organizations should not be capitalized: *the United Nations, the Police Athletic League.*)

2. Capitalize the first word of every sentence, including the first word of every quoted sentence:

    He said proudly, "Everything is in order."

3. For titles of books, articles, movies, and plays, always capitalize the first word and every word except small prepositions, conjunctions, and articles of four letters or less: *The Old Man and the Sea; Much Ado About Nothing; Life with Father.*

CASE

Use the correct case of the pronoun (either the subjective case, the objective case, or the possessive case). For *nouns* in the possessive case look up how to use the apostrophe under PUNCTUATION.

A hint for speedy correction: Here is a list of the problem-pronouns in all their three cases. Pick out the pronoun you have misused and note what case it is in. Obviously the correct form must be one of the other two case-forms. Look up the examples of *errors* given for these other two case-forms, and you will find one similar to your own as well as the correct form you should use. Here are the six troublesome pronouns and their cases:

Subjective case:	I	we	he	she	they	who
Objective case:	me	us	him	her	them	whom
Possessive case:	my	our	his	her	their	whose

Note: If the error you have is *it* or *it's,* change the word to *its* (the correct spelling of the possessive case). The spelling *it's* is the contraction of *it is.*

1. SUBJECTIVE CASE.

If the pronoun is grammatically the *subject* of the sentence or clause, then keep it in the *subjective* case.

Error: My brother and *me* double-date very often.
Correction: I. ("My brother and I" is the subject. Would you say, "*Me* double-date"?) **My brother and I double-date very often.**

Error: If anyone deserved to win, it was *her.*
Correction: *she.* (In the above construction—*it* + form of the verb *to be* + pronoun—we have a special problem. In speech, the pronoun is likely to be heard in the objective case: "It's *me,*" "It was *her,*" "It may be *them.*" In formal writing, however, if you cannot avoid the construction alto-

gether, you must use the more apparently stilted subjective case: It is *I;* It was *she;* It may be *they.*) If anyone deserved to win, it was *she.*

Error: She was as tall as *him.*
Correction: *he.* (Think of the sentence in this way: She was as tall as he [was]. *He* is the subject of an understood verb, *was.*) She was as tall as he. (Some writers, to avoid sounding stilted, would prefer *He and she are the same height.*)

Error: We climbed faster than *them.*
Correction: *they.* (Here again, there is an understood verb: We climbed faster than they [did].) We climbed faster than *they.*

Error: I enjoy speaking to *whom*ever wants to learn mechanics.
Correction: *who*ever. (Remember that the object of the preposition *to* is not *whomever,* or even *whoever,* but the whole clause, "whoever wants to learn mechanics." *Who*ever is naturally the subject of this clause, and *wants* is the verb. *The case of the pronoun is decided solely by the pronoun's position inside its own clause.* Very simply, you wouldn't say, "*Whom* wants"; you would say, "*Who* wants.") **I enjoy speaking to whoever wants to learn mechanics.**

Error: He revealed *whom* he thought would win.
Correction: *who.* (The writer here may have been fooled by two things: 1. He may have thought that *whom* is the object of the verb *revealed.* The object, however, is the whole clause "who he thought would win." 2. The writer may have thought that *whom* was a direct object in its *own* clause. He was fooled by the words "he thought," which is a parenthetical expression that comes between the true subject-verb combination, *who would win.* See further examples in the following discussion of the objective case.) **He revealed who he thought would win.**

2. OBJECTIVE CASE.

If the pronoun is the object of a verb or of a preposition, then keep it in the *objective* case.

Error: The fire was put out by us, Jim and *I.*
Correction: *me.* (*Me,* just like *us,* is in the objective case after the preposition *by.*) **The fire was put out by us, Jim and me.**

Error: I was not sure *who* she liked.
Correction: *whom.* (Rearrange the sentence to see clearly

the subject-verb-object pattern: She liked *whom. Whom* is object of the verb *liked.*) **I was not sure whom she liked.**

Error: Nobody knew *who* he was talking about.
Correction: *whom.* (In the whole clause, "whom he was talking about," *whom* is the object of the preposition *about.* Rearrange the clause to see the pattern clearly: He was talking about *whom.*) **Nobody knew whom he was talking about.**

3. POSSESSIVE CASE.

The use of the possessive pronoun before the gerund often gives students trouble.

Error: I did not approve of *him* going by himself.
Correction: *his.* (A pronoun that comes directly before a gerund—a verbal used as a noun—is ordinarily in the possessive case. In the example, *going* is a gerund.) **I did not approve of his going by himself.** (For the possessive case of *nouns,* see APOSTROPHE.)

---

choppy CHOPPY SENTENCES

Revise your series of short, choppy sentences by varying your sentence patterns. Do not simply combine your sentences with "ands" or semicolons. The result of that would be a series of *longer* choppy sentences. If you master the very simple art of using a variety of sentence types, your style will become much smoother and your grade will improve considerably.

Choppy: She had a very good coat. It was with her almost everywhere. It was a dark-blue woollen coat with a blue lining. It was full-length and conservative-looking. At one time it had a belt, but that was later lost. On the sleeves some worn spots were starting to appear. They showed how much she used it. It kept her warm on cold nights, and that was what counted most.

Smoother: She had a very good coat *that* she took with her almost everywhere. Conservative-looking, it was a full-length, dark-blue woollen *garment* with a blue lining. *In spite of* losing the belt, she used the coat *so much that* worn spots were starting to appear on the sleeves. *As far as she was concerned,* what counted most was that it kept her warm on cold nights.

Analysis: A choppy paragraph of eight sentences is re-written to form a much smoother paragraph of four sentences that is slightly shorter (68 words versus 72 for the choppy version), even though two new phrases have been added. In the revised paragraph, the italicized words and phrases are added elements that do not appear in the original. For the most part, they reveal logical relationships between thoughts, relationships which are not clearly seen in the original. Revising choppy writing is not simply a matter of combining short sentences into longer ones, but of using the resources of phrasing and sentence structure *to reveal logical relationships between thoughts.* The main techniques of revision used above are discussed in detail under SUBORDINATION, TRANSITIONS, and VARIETY IN SENTENCE PATTERNS.

cliché

CLICHÉS

Avoid using "clichés"—expressions which are so commonly used that they have lost the original flavor and vividness they once possessed. The overuse of clichés implies lazy, unoriginal thinking. (See also TRITENESS.)

Examples of clichés (italicized):

He wanted to live out in *the wide open spaces.*
They made progress *by leaps and bounds.*
On picnics one can relax and enjoy *Mother Nature.*
I felt *as cool as a cucumber.*
No one suspected the *trials and tribulations* they went through.
Her cousin was *as quiet as a mouse.*

COHERENCE

Completely rewrite the indicated passage. As it now stands, the material does not make clear, logical sense on a first reading. The parts are not coherently organized to follow one another in a logical pattern.

Suggestion for revision: Clarify in your own mind the ideas you wanted to express. Then imagine yourself attempting to explain these ideas as clearly as possible to a friend who knows nothing of the subject, or to a younger brother or sister. If you put yourself fully into this dramatic situation, there is no doubt that you will clear up the lack of coherence in your writing.

A SAMPLE PARAGRAPH LACKING COHERENCE:

In "Song of Myself," Walt Whitman speaks of his feelings toward nature and life in all its aspects. He loves anything that is unlimited by conventions and expresses itself freely. He can only feel a liking toward limited things. Love, for him, is the greatest form of awareness. "Never let anything put you into a rut" seems to be his motto.

17

The above paragraph is a typically incoherent piece of writing. Not only is there a lack of logical continuity from one sentence to another, but the fog and confusion is made murkier by phrasing, as in the third sentence ("He can only feel a liking . . ."), which says just the opposite of what the writer meant. In addition, this paragraph commits the typical error of omitting necessary steps in the logical sequence of ideas, so that one thought appears to have nothing to do with the next. (See also PARAGRAPH-ING.)

THE SAME PARAGRAPH MADE COHERENT—
AND NECESSARILY LONGER:

In "Song of Myself," Walt Whitman speaks of his boundless love for nature, a concept which includes all things that exist. He loves especially anything or anyone who expresses his inmost drives freely and does not allow himself to be limited by deadening conventions. He acclaims the force of love in the universe as a whole, for love destroys all limiting conventions and leads us to freedom by giving us greater and greater awareness of ourselves and the world about us. Whitman can feel only sympathy, not love, for people limited by tradition and custom. He would prefer that we kept this motto in mind: "Never let anything put you into a rut." (Of course, it would now be better not to include the last sentence with its shabby "motto.")

COLON :

Place the colon after an introductory statement to call attention to what follows, such as an explanation, a list of items, or a long quotation. See the following examples:

1. COLON INTRODUCING AN EXPLANATION.

Here is my honest opinion: I think you are a crackpot. (When a full sentence follows a colon, you may capitalize the first word or not, as you please. If a *quoted* sentence follows the colon, you *must* begin the sentence with a capital letter. EXAMPLE: The sign was all too clear: "No swimming in this area.")

2. COLON BEFORE A LIST OF ITEMS.

Be sure to take the following things with you on a long ocean voyage: plenty of books, a deck of cards, a chess set, and a warm blanket.

Misuse of colon: On a long ocean voyage be sure to take along: plenty of books, a deck of cards, a chess set, and a warm blanket. (There is no natural pause after "along," as there is after "voyage" in the previous example. Do not use the colon to interrupt the normal flow of the sentence.)

3. COLON BEFORE A LONG QUOTATION.

In "An Apology for Idlers," Robert Louis Stevenson says: "There is a sort of dead-alive, hackneyed people about, who are scarcely conscious of living except in the exercise of some conventional occupation. Bring these fellows into the country, or set them aboard ship, and you will see how they pine for their desk or their study."

C   COMMA

The following five directions for using the comma will solve practically all the comma problems you will ever have.

1. Use the comma before coordinating conjunctions *(and, but, or, nor, for)* **that join two main clauses.**

Examples:

I completely forgot about our date for last night, *and* I sincerely hope that you will try to understand.

Stop going with other girls behind my back, *or* I promise I'll never see you again.

Exception: If the main clauses are very short, you do not have to separate them with a comma. As an example, take the boy's obvious reply to the girl's ultimatum:

I never have *and* I never will.

2. Use the comma after sentence elements that appear before the main clause, such as subordinate clauses and phrases.

Examples:

When he spoke to the student, the instructor asked him whether he studied very much.
Shaking his head, the student replied that his brothers kept the TV blaring day and night.
As a solution to the problem, the instructor recommended the temporary removal of a few tubes from the set.

Exception: Most very short prepositional phrases that come before a main clause are not followed by a comma:

After a moment the student admitted that TV wasn't his only distraction from studying.

But certain introductory words and phrases, like *for example, in short, in fact, however, consequently,* are used to form a bridge, or transition, from one sentence to another, and are always followed by a comma (See TRANSITIONS):

In conclusion, we all had a merry time.

NOTE: If a subordinate clause *follows* the main clause, do *not* separate them with a comma:

No fishing boats ventured out that day because the water was too rough. (No comma between *day* and the subordinate clause beginning with *because*.)

3. Use commas to set off parenthetical sentence elements.

A sentence element is parenthetical, or *nonrestrictive,* if it supplies information not essential to the clear meaning of the sentence.

In the following examples, the nonrestrictive elements are italicized.

Examples:

Modern automobiles, *which at last have gotten rid of their tail fins*, strike me as more attractive than the older models.
He is, *I am sure*, a good sport.
They are gone, *thank goodness*.

Test for parenthetical elements: To test whether an element is parenthetical, remove it from the sentence. If the basic idea of the sentence remains the same, and is not distorted, then the element you have removed is parenthetical and should be set off by commas. Read the above examples without the words in italics, and you will find that the ideas of the original sentences remain unchanged.

Restrictive elements: Restrictive sentence elements are necessary to the meaning of the sentence, as in this example:

All men *who are hard of hearing* should wear hearing aids.

Notice that the clause "who are hard of hearing" is *essential* to the meaning of the sentence. If you remove it, the basic idea of the sentence is distorted. Restrictive elements, as you can see, are not set apart from the rest of the sentence by commas.

4. Use commas between items in a series.

A series consists of three or more elements, which may be single *words, phrases,* or *clauses* (these last three italicized words are in a series).

Examples:

The basement was *dark, damp,* and *cold*. (The formula for the series is *a, b,* and *c*. Also winning acceptance in formal writing is the formula *a, b* and *c*, where there is no comma between the last two items in the series: The basement was *dark, damp* and *cold*.)

He stumbled *down the stairs, across the room,* and *through the doorway*. (A series of three prepositional phrases.)

I asked them *when I could come, where I could stay,* and *what I could do.* (A series of three subordinate clauses.)

I whistled shrilly, I listened in vain, and I turned sadly away. (Three main clauses, if they are very short, may be connected in a series by commas.)

5. Use commas between coordinate adjectives that come before a noun.

Examples:

She is an *old, faithful* servant.
Look at his *clear, twinkling* eyes.

The test for coordinate adjectives is to insert the word *and* between them and omit the comma. If the adjectives are coordinate (equal in rank), you will feel no awkwardness in reading them: *clear and twinkling* eyes.

The test shows that the following examples are not coordinate adjectives: a *small living* room, a *little old* man. The last adjectve in each pair is really treated as part of the noun. It would be awkward to say "a small and living room," or "a little and old man." Where you can insert the *and,* use the comma. Where you cannot insert the *and,* omit the comma.

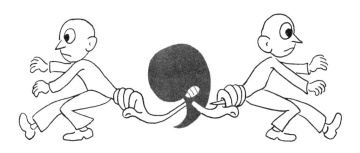

COMMA SPLICE

Do not join, or "splice," two separate sentences with a comma. **Change the comma to a period (or to a semicolon, if you are certain how to use it: see SEMICOLON).** The comma splice, a type of RUN-ON SENTENCE, seriously handicaps the reader by preventing him from distinguishing between the end of one *thought* and the beginning of the next.

Comma Splice: New York is a busy industrial city, thousands of cars, trucks, and buses move through it every day.
Revision: Change the comma after *city* to a period and capitalize *thousands,* which is now the first word of a new sentence. You could also correct the error by changing the comma after *city* to a semicolon [;]. **New York is a busy industrial city. Thousands of cars, trucks, and buses move through it every day.** [*Or*] **New York is a busy industrial city; thousands of cars, trucks, and buses move through it every day.**

A second type of comma splice error is made in the case of sentences beginning with words such as *therefore, however, then, nevertheless, moreover, also, still, thus,* or with expressions such as *in fact, for example, that is, on the other hand, in other words.* These are transitional words or phrases which begin a new main clause or a new sentence. Most often the main clause beginning with such an expression should be linked with the previous main clause by a semicolon. Study the following examples:

Comma Splice: We packed all our luggage, then we were on our way to the airport.
Revision: Change the comma after *luggage* to a semicolon. **We packed all our luggage; then we were on our way to the airport.**

Comma Splice: He did not arrive in time, therefore we had no choice but to leave without him.
Revision: Place a semicolon after *time*. **He did not arrive in time; therefore we had no choice but to leave without him.**

Comma Splice: I have always loved sports, in fact, I was once the youngest member of my team in the Little League.
Revision: Place a semicolon after *sports*. **I have always loved sports; in fact, I was once the youngest member of my team in the Little League.**

---

comp   COMPARISON

Add the word or words needed to complete the comparison. Incomplete comparisons appear to be absurd or illogical statements. (See also MIXED METAPHORS.)

Illogical: The traffic in New York City is worse than Chicago.
Revised: *Traffic* is illogically compared to a city!) **The traffic in New York City is worse than** *the traffic* **in Chicago.**

Illogical: In this poem, Robert Frost expresses ideas different from most other poets.
Revised: (In the error, *ideas* are illogically compared to *poets*.) **In this poem, Robert Frost expresses ideas different from** *those of* **most other poets.**

Incomplete: The salesman's income was at least as high, if not higher than, the branch manager's.
Revised: (Complete the phrase: "as high *as*.") The salesman's income was at least as high *as,* if not higher than, the branch manager's.

DANGLING MODIFIER

The modifier in your sentence "dangles" because it does not clearly and logically relate to another word in the sentence. **Rewrite the sentence** in either of two ways: 1) Change the dangling element into a subordinate clause by adding a subject and verb, or 2) Change the main clause so that the subject agrees with the dangling modifier.

Dangling modifiers appear in italics in the following examples:

Dangling: *When sitting,* my shoulders tend to slump back. ("I," the logical subject of the modifier, does not appear in the sentence. As now written, the sentence says "my shoulders" are sitting.)

Revision: 1. Change the dangling element into a subordinate clause: *When I sit,* **my shoulders tend to slump back.** 2. Change the subject of the main clause to agree with the dangling element: **When sitting,** *I* **find that my shoulders tend to slump back.**

Dangling: *To type well,* your legs must be in the correct position. (Are "your legs" doing the typing?)

Revision: 1. *If you want to type well,* **your legs must be in the correct position.** 2. **To type well,** *you must keep* **your legs in the correct position.**

Dangling: *Going home,* it started to drizzle. (Where is the subject who is "going"?)

Revision: 1. *As I was going home,* **it started to drizzle.** 2. **Going home,** *I felt it starting* **to drizzle.**

dash	# DASH —

For the most part, avoid using the dash if commas or parentheses will serve equally well. Use the dash to mark an abrupt shift in thought, or to set off a parenthetical element that you wish to make emphatic. NOTE: Most typewriters are equipped with only a hyphen and not a dash. To type the dash, use two strokes of the hyphen key [--].

Examples:

"I would like—no, as a matter of fact, I wouldn't." (Abrupt shift in thought.)
I must admit—since you force me to tell you—that my opinion of you is not very high. (Dashes set off a parenthetical element emphatically. Parentheses seem to muffle and make unemphatic the material they enclose.)

D	# DICTION

Change the word or phrase you have used to one that is more exact in *meaning,* or to one that is more appropriate in *tone* to the rest of the composition.

Certain errors in diction recur so frequently that it might be worth your while to check your error against the *Glossary of Common Errors in Diction* that has been arranged alphabetically below. In any case, take the following two suggestions as a guide for correcting and avoiding mistakes in diction:

1. Check on the exact meaning of the word you have used in a large (at least desk-sized) modern dictionary. You may find that in some cases your spelling is to blame, as in the confusion of *accept* with *except*. The most common errors are treated below in the *Glossary*.

2. Check in your dictionary to see whether the word you have used is considered slang, or colloquial, or perhaps nonstandard and therefore out of place in the formal style of standard written English that is generally demanded of you. If the particular usage of a word is "standard" (generally acceptable in cultivated speaking and writing), it will not be labeled. But there may be other definitions of the word listed, and these will be labeled in various ways: for example, as *slang, colloq.* (colloquial), *nonstandard, illit.* (illiterate).

GLOSSARY OF COMMON ERRORS IN DICTION

Accept, except. Do not confuse these words. The meaning of *accept* is "to receive" or "to agree to" something: "I accepted his offer." *Except,* used as a verb, can only mean "to exclude": "He was excepted from the list of prize winners."

Ad. In formal English, use the full word *advertisement.*

Affect, effect. Do not confuse these words. As a verb, "to affect" means "to influence": "His speech affected many people." "To effect" means "to bring about," or "to cause": "It is hard to effect a change in society." When you incorrectly use *affect* as a noun, change it to *effect,* which means "result": "The effect of the blow was to split the stone in half."

Aggravate. "Aggravate" means "to make worse." It is not a synonym for "irritate" or "annoy." Do not write: "His snide remarks *aggravated* me." Write: "His snide remarks *irritated* me." Further insults would, of course, *aggravate* your irritated condition.

Allusion, illusion. An *allusion* is an indirect reference, but an *illusion* is a false or deceptive notion.

Alright. This is still an unacceptable spelling of *all right*.

Among, between. Ordinarily, *between* is used when only two items are spoken of: "I divided the food between the cat and the dog." *Among* relates to more than two items: "The prize money was divided among the three winners."

Amount, number. When things or people can be counted individually, use *number:* "There was a large number of students in the hall." When you are referring to a quantity of something which is not thought of in terms of individual, countable units, use *amount:* "A large amount of gold was discovered in the mountain."

Anyways, anywheres. Use the standard forms, *anyway* and *anywhere*.

Around. Do not use the colloquial "around" in expressions like "He left *around* ten o'clock," or, "I can recite *around* fifteen poems." Use "about": "He left *about* ten o'clock." "I can recite *about* fifteen poems."

As. *As* in the sense of "because" is often not as clear as *because, for,* or *since.* "I would like to leave because (not *as*) I'm tired." See also **Like.**

At. See **Where at.**

Awhile, a while. After a preposition, spell as two words: "I slept for a while." Otherwise spell as one word: "I slept awhile."

Because. See **Reason is because.**

Being as, being that. *Because* or *since* are preferred in Standard English.

Beside, besides. *Beside* means "at the side of"; *besides* means "in addition to." "*Besides* chicken, we ate roast beef and bananas as we sat *beside* the stream."

Bust, busted. These are slang forms of the verb *burst.* Use *burst* in present and past tenses. *Bursted* does not exist.

Compare to, compare with. *To compare to* means to state that something is *similar to* something else which is really quite different: "He compared the coffee *to* mud." *To compare with* means to investigate the similarities and differences between two things that are of a like order: "He compared the female students *with* the male students and found the females brighter."

Complected. Nonstandard for *complexioned.*

Could of. Illiterate for *could have,* which in speech is often contracted to *could've* and misspelled *could of.* (As a general rule, avoid contractions in formal writing.)

Data. This word is a Latin plural (singular, *datum*) and is often used in English with plural verbs and pronouns: "*These* data *are* out of date." Many educated people equally accept its use in the singular: "*This* data *is* no longer useful." (See Strata, Phenomena.)

Don't is a contraction of *do not* and must not be confused with *does not* or *doesn't.* NONSTANDARD: "He don't mind insults." STANDARD: "He *doesn't* (or *does not*) mind insults." Bear in mind that contractions are acceptable in speech, but not in formal writing.

Effect. See **Affect.**

Enthuse. In formal English, it is better to use *to become enthusiastic.*

Equally as good. Drop the *as* and write "equally good," or use "just as good."

Except. See **Accept.**

Farther, further. *Farther* is often preferred to express extent in *space,* whereas *further* is preferred to express extent in *time* or *degree:* "We walked *farther* into the woods"; "He went *further* in condemning him than anyone expected."

Fewer, less. When referring to separate items that can be counted, use *fewer:* "You make *fewer* mistakes now than when you started." *Less* refers to the degree or amount of something we consider as a whole, and not as a series of individual items: "I have *less* money now than when I started."

Hadn't ought. Nonstandard. Instead of saying, "I hadn't ought to have gone," say, **"I shouldn't have gone."**

Healthful, healthy. The usual preference is that whatever *gives* health is *healthful* ("a healthful climate") and that whatever *has* health is healthy ("a healthy person").

Illusion. See **Allusion.**

In regards to. Use *in regard to.*

Irregardless. The proper form is *regardless.*

It's. A contraction of *it is* and a frequent misspelling of the possessive pronoun *its:* He examined *its* (not *it's*) contents.

Kind of, sort of. In standard written English, change this expression to *somewhat, rather, a little:* "I was somewhat (not *kind of*) annoyed."

Lay, lie. When you mean "to put," use *lay.* The forms of "to lay" are "I *lay* the book down" (present), "I *laid* the book down" (past), and "I *have laid* the book down" (present perfect). When you mean "to recline," use lie. The forms of "to lie" are "I *lie* in my bed" (present), "I *lay* in my bed" (past), and "I *have lain* in my bed" (present perfect).

Less. See **Fewer.**

Like, as, as if. *Like* is a preposition and is properly used in phrases *like* this or the following: "He looks *like* my father." It is improperly used when followed by a clause. MISUSE: "It looks *like* my father enjoys your company." REVISION: Change *like* to *as if.* **"It looks as if my father enjoys your company."** In the sentence, "I behaved *like* I was told to," change *like* to *as.* **"I behaved as I was told to."**

May of, might of. Illiterate for *may have, might have.* See **Could of.**

Mighty. Use a standard word like *very:* "I was very (not *mighty*) tired."

Most. Use *almost:* "I saw him almost (not *most*) every day."

Must of. Illiterate for *must have.* See **Could of.**

Nice. A word expressing a vaguely favorable attitude toward something. Avoid it in formal writing by using a more exact word.

Of. Illiterate for *have* in *could of, might of,* etc. See **Could of.**

Off of. Drop the *of.*

Phenomena. In formal English, *phenomena* is the plural, *phenomenon* the singular.

Quite. Do not overuse to mean *very,* as in "quite good," "quite hard," etc.

Real. Keep expressions like "real good," "real exciting," out of your written English. Use "*really* good" or "*very* good."

Reason is because. In informal usage one hears: "The *reason* I told you *is because* I can trust you." For formal writing, revise as follows: METHOD 1. Change *because* to *that* ("The reason I told you is *that* I can trust you"). METHOD 2. Recast the sentence ("I told you because I can trust you").

Should of. Illiterate for *should have.* See **Could of.**

So. 1. Do not overuse *so* as a conjunction joining main clauses. See **Subordination.**

2. Do not use *so* where you could use *so that:* Change "I came to visit you *so* we could have a chat" to **"I came to visit you *so that* we could have a chat."**

3. Do not overuse *so* as a "feminine intensive": "I was so disappointed." "She is so nice, isn't she?" Try substituting *very,* or *extremely.*

Sort of. See **Kind of.**

Strata. The singular is *stratum.* Use *strata* only as a plural.

Sure. Use *certainly,* or *surely:* "I certainly (not *sure*) was tired."

Try and. Substitute *try to.*

Where at. In a sentence like "I know where he is at," *at* is unnecessary and should be dropped. **"I know where he is."**

Which, who. Use *who* (or *that*), but never use *which* to refer to persons. "Here is the man who (not *which*) is responsible."

While. This is mainly a conjunction of time: "I ran while I still had time." Do not overwork it to mean *and, but,* or *whereas:* "I loved roses, but (not *while*) she preferred daisies."

Would of. Illiterate for *would have.* See **Could of.**

.../ ELLIPSIS ...

In formal writing, the ellipsis—three double-spaced periods—is used only to show that you have omitted material from a quoted passage.

Example:

> "Poetry turns all things to loveliness; it exalts the beauty of that which is most beautiful, and it adds beauty to that which is most deformed; . . . it subdues to union . . . all irreconcilable things."
>
> —Percy Bysshe Shelley

NOTE: To show that you are omitting one or more whole paragraphs from a quoted passage of prose, or that you are cutting at least a full line from quoted poetry, use a full line of periods:

What thou lovest well remains,
. . . .
What thou lov'st well is thy true heritage

> —Ezra Pound

em EMPHASIS

1. Rearrange your sentence to give the important words and phrases their proper emphasis. The position of greatest emphasis is the *end* of your sentence. Next in emphasis is the beginning of your sentence.

2. Change the weak *passive* voice of the verb to the strong *active* voice.

3. Underline a word or phrase for strong emphasis, but use this method sparingly.

1. EMPHASIS THROUGH PROPER WORD ORDER.

Poor emphasis: We jammed into the car and started on our trip *in the morning, just after the sun rose.* (The italicized phrases are the least important elements of the sentence, but are placed at the end, the position of *most* emphasis.)

Proper emphasis: In the morning, just after the sun rose, we jammed into the car and started on our trip. (The main clause, beginning "We jammed," is now properly emphasized.)

2. EMPHASIS THROUGH ACTIVE VOICE.

Unemphatic passive voice: At camp, many games were played by the children which were not played at home.

Emphatic active voice: At camp, the children played many games which they did not play at home.

3. UNDERLINING FOR STRONG EMPHASIS.

Remember that underlined words in a manuscript appear in italics *(slant type like this)* in print. Underline a word or phrase for strong emphasis only if you can not achieve such emphasis by rephrasing or rearranging sentence parts.

Example:

It is of course *possible* that all or any of our beliefs may be mistaken. . . . But we cannot have *reason* to reject a belief except on the ground of some other belief.

—Bertrand Russell

!/   EXCLAMATION POINT !

The exclamation point is used to express *strong* feeling. Do not overuse it.

Examples:

What a wonderful, wonderful day! (Exuberance.)
Get out of here! (A brisk command.)

frag   FRAGMENTARY SENTENCE

You have written only a phrase or a subordinate clause, or some other *piece* of a sentence, but not a full sentence. If you can logically attach what you have written to the previous or the following sentence, do so. If not, then expand your fragment into a full sentence by adding the missing element(s).

In certain types of creative writing, fragments are used effectively to suggest the frequently rapid and non-grammatical flow of human thought, especially at emotional high points. But in formal, expository writing, where logic and calm are supposed to prevail, sentence fragments are rarely appropriate.

In the following examples, unjustifiable sentence fragments are in italics:

Fragment: I do not have the steadiest hand in the world. *As you can see from my writing.*
Revision: (The fragment is a subordinate clause that is non-restrictive, and should be attached to the previous sentence by a comma.) I do not have the steadiest hand in the world, as you can see from my writing.

Fragment: He spent some of the best years of his life in Tucson. *A city where the weather is springlike eight months of the year.*
Revision: (The fragment is an appositive, a noun—*city*—which renames or identifies a previous noun—*Tuscon.* Join the appositive to the first part of the sentence with a comma.) He spent some of the best years of his life in Tucson, a city where the weather is springlike eight months of the year.

Fragment: He lectured on many interesting things. *For example, about magic.*
Revision: (The fragment is a phrase. It is better style to make a complete sentence out of it than to add it to the previous sentence.) He lectured on many interesting things. For example, *he spoke* about magic. (Better yet, however, would be to recast the entire idea: He lectured on magic and many other interesting things.)

Fragment: John would not make a good captain. *A good player, yes, but not always a good sport.*
Revision: (The fragment here is the complement of a subject and verb which were both omitted. Supply them.) John would not make a good captain. *He is* a good player, yes, but not always a good sport.

hy   HYPHEN -

Insert a hyphen (-) where indicated. The hyphen is mainly used to connect words that are to be regarded as a unit of meaning: *fire-eater, home-brew, sit-in.* (In many cases, usage is not generally agreed upon. In case of doubt, consult a recent dictionary.)

The following examples illustrate special uses of hyphens, such as in preventing misreading and in end-of-line word-division.

1. Hyphens connecting words before a noun:

an intelligent-looking face
nineteenth-century history (But not in "the history of the nineteenth century.)
a do-or-die attitude
behind-the-scenes dealings (But in the sentence "There were shady dealings going on behind the scenes" no hyphens are used because "behind the scenes" comes *after* the noun.)
four-, six-, and eight-cylinder cars (Note that sometimes hyphens "dangle" in a series before a noun.)

2. Hyphens to prevent misreading:

a foreign-car salesman (Unless you mean *a foreign car-salesman,* a Frenchman, for example, who sells cars in his native Paris.)
a small-appliances store (Such a store could be very large, indeed, but nobody would believe it if you removed the hyphen!)
They *re-covered* the chair. (Compare: They *recovered* the stolen chair.)

3. Hyphens for numbers between twenty and one hundred:

twenty-nine, sixty-two, eighty-eight (See also **NUMBERS.**)

4. Hyphens for end-of-line word-division:

hyphen-ation, not *hyphe-nation* (Divide words at the end of a full syllable. A good dictionary prints word-entries in a way that shows their syllable structure: for example, sym·pa·thet·ic.)

inc   INCOMPLETE CONSTRUCTION

Add the word or words necessary to complete the construction you now have. Examples:

Preposition omitted: She was greatly interested and enthusiastic about the project.
Revised: She was greatly interested *in* and enthusiastic about about the project.

Verb omitted: The people were all interesting and my vacation, in general, wonderful.
Revised: The people were all interesting and my vacation, in general, *was* wonderful. The plural verb *were,* used with *people,* cannot agree with the singular noun *vacation.*)

Verb omitted: We never have and never shall attack without provocation.
Revised: We never have *attacked* and never shall attack without provocation. The auxiliary verb *have* must be followed by *attacked.*)

See COMPARISONS for other examples of incomplete constructions.

ital   ITALICS

1. Underline the titles of books, magazines, newspapers, plays, and movies. Do not put quotation marks around them: The Atlantic Monthly, The Return of the Native, King Lear.

2. Underline foreign words and expressions: coup d'état, comme il faut, persona non grata.

3. Underline words or letters if they are not used for their meaning, but as words or letters only: Add a <u>u</u> to <u>gaze</u> and you get <u>gauze</u>.

4. Underline words when strong emphasis is desired: "I'm leaving <u>now</u>," she declared, "<u>not</u> tomorrow!"

NOTE: Underlined words appear, when printed, in italic or slanted type, *like this.*

lc LOWER-CASE

Do not capitalize the word or words indicated. Lower-case in printing pertains to small letters as opposed to capitals. (See CAPITALIZATION.)

mod MISPLACED MODIFIER

1. Place the word or phrase marked as misplaced in a closer or clearer relation to the word it modifies.

2. Do not awkwardly split infinitives.

1. MISPLACED MODIFIERS.

Misplaced: I *only* know one thing.
Better: I know *only* one thing.

Misplaced: The emperor was just and kind to people *in his way.*

Better: (The student's error makes it seem as if the emperor were kind to his enemies!) *In his way,* the emperor was just and kind to people.

Misplaced: He fell while he was running *into a manhole.*
Better: He fell *into a manhole* while he was running.

Misplaced: The man who was working *quickly* swallowed his lunch.
Better: This is a case of a "squinting" modifier. Does *quickly* modify *working* or *swallowed*? If it modifies *swallowed,* then write: The man who was working swallowed his lunch *quickly.*

2. AWKWARDLY SPLIT INFINITIVES.

Split infinitives that read *smoothly* are now acceptable in formal writing:

Acceptable: He managed *to* completely *undermine* the proceedings.
Unacceptable: He foolishly tried *to,* without studying at all, *pass* the Chemistry I final.
Improved: Without studying at all, he foolishly tried *to pass* the Chemistry I final.

mx	MIXED CONSTRUCTION

You began your sentence with one construction or figure of speech, then shifted to another which cannot logically or grammatically complete the sentence. Change one part of the sentence so that it harmonizes with the rest.

Examples:

Mixed sentence parts: Learning to love the beauty of nature, the endless variety of things around you, the air itself, and you will be a complete person.
Correction: Change *learning* to *learn*. **Learn to love the beauty of nature, the endless variety of things around you, the air itself, and you will be a complete person.**

Mixed sentence parts: By throwing the upper right-hand lever is the way to stop the machine.
Correction: Drop the first word, *by*. **Throwing the upper right-hand lever is the way to stop the machine.** (If the writer wants to keep the beginning of his sentence, he will have to change the end: **By throwing the upper right-hand lever** *one stops* **the machine.**)

Mixed sentence parts: I bought a picture which, in hanging it upside down, made no difference in the effect it made.

Correction: (The main grammatical confusion lies in the *which* clause, "which . . . made no difference in the effect it made." The pronoun *which* stands for the noun *picture,* and so the clause illogically says, "the *picture* made no difference in the effect it made.") **I bought a picture which could be hung upside down without any difference in the effect it made.**

Mixed metaphors: The wheels of fate moved their grimy *hands.* (Since when do wheels have hands? As you can see, mixing figures of speech can result in an absurd, illogical image—funny, but not intentionally so.)

Mixed metaphors: A tongue of land jutted out from the foot of the cliff. (It is absurd to imagine a foot sticking out its tongue.

No ¶   NO PARAGRAPH

Do not begin a new paragraph at this point. (See PARAGRAPHING.)

No P   NO PUNCTUATION

Do not insert any punctuation at this point.

num   NUMBERS

Spell out any figures that can be spoken in one or two words. Use numerals for any sum that must be expressed in three or more words.

Examples:

thirty, fifty-five, 172.

¶   PARAGRAPHING

Begin a new paragraph at the place marked. The first line of a paragraph is *indented,* that is, begins several spaces to the right of where a line usually begins.

A paragraph is a division of a composition, a part of a whole. A paragraph does not begin anywhere you please, but only at the point where you are shifting to a distinctly new part of the whole subject being explored. In writing and re-reading what you have written, try to detect these major shifting points.

In formal essay writing, a paragraph normally consists of at *least* two sentences, and of at *least* fifty words (a very rough guide, not to be applied mechanically!). One sentence, usually the first, is the "topic" sentence and states the general idea of the paragraph. The other sentences should stick to the "topic" and develop the main idea through details, or examples, or logical argument.

Each sentence should flow from the previous sentence and lead to the following one in a clear, smooth, and logical manner (see COHERENCE and TRANSITIONS).

Keep in mind your main idea and avoid unrelated statements if you want to avoid damaging the unity of your paragraph. At the same time, you owe it to your reader to *develop* your paragraph sufficiently. Be certain to give enough information to "cover" the topic. If you do not have enough to say, then either you need to do more thinking about your material or else the topic is too unimportant to deserve development in a paragraph of its own. If the topic is not worth developing, then either fit it smoothly into another paragraph where it logically belongs, or get rid of it altogether. Do not, however, get rid of material simply because you do not know how to develop it or do not want to be bothered!

Here is a paragraph, written by a student, in which the first sentence states the topic and the following sentences *develop* the topic sufficiently through illustrative detail:

> You will see only the hardiest citizens among us greeting the cold weather with a welcoming smile. If you watch through an unfrosted corner of your window, you will see them striding briskly along, rosy-cheeked, and breathing in deeply the chill air. No gloves cover their ruddy knuckles, no scarves wrap their necks, and no ear-muffs strifle the angry whistling of the wind that to their ears is as sweet as birdsong. They walk along in light jackets, their shirts open at the neck, as if this were as balmy a day as any in the year.

// PARALLELISM

Keep sentence elements of equal importance in parallel form. Parallel form is the balancing of equal grammatical structures against one another: for example, noun against noun, active verb against active verb, infinitive against infinitive, phrase against phrase, clause against clause.

Notice the method of improving parallelism in the following examples:

Poor: I enjoy going to movies, listening to music, and cards.
Improved: I enjoy going to movies, listening to music, and *playing* **cards.** (A parallel -*ing* word is needed before cards.)

Poor: She learned to type up reports, to file correspondence, and how to smile pleasantly.
Improved: She learned to type up reports, to file correspondence, and *to smile* **pleasantly.** (The "how" upsets the pattern of three parallel infinitives.)

Poor: The opinion of one off-beat columnist is that the mayor is adept at underhand dealings profitable only to himself, and we should therefore throw him out of office.
Improved: The opinion of one off-beat columnist is that the mayor is adept at underhand dealings profitable only to himself, and *that* **we should therefore throw him out of office.** (The second "that" makes it clear that the opinion which follows is solely the columnist's and does not belong to the

writer of the sentence. You can see how important clear parallelism can be!)

Poor: He always plays the piano with ease, with confidence,
and takes pleasure in it.
Improved: **He always plays the piano with ease, with confidence, and** *with pleasure.* (We now have a series of parallel
prepositional phrases.)

PARENTHESES ()

Use parentheses to enclose material that is clearly
supplementary and not essential to the meaning of the
sentence. Whatever is enclosed in parentheses appears relatively unimportant to the reader. Use parentheses very
sparingly; never use them when you can use commas
instead.

Examples of the effective use of parentheses:

I walked right up to him (no one was with him at the time)
and told him what we had decided.
Last week he came up with a brilliant new idea (the seeds of it
had been ripening in his mind for months) only to see it
rejected as absurd by the committee.

Ineffective use of parentheses:

His brother told him (John) not to annoy him (Allen) any-
more. (You cannot compensate for poor reference of pronouns by using explanatory parentheses. The sentence would
have to be rewritten for smoothness of style *and* clear meaning as well.)

Some critics think that atmospheric pollution (not the popula-
tion explosion) is the more serious challenge to mankind's
survival. (Commas serve better than parentheses to set off
this relatively important part of the sentence.)

PASSIVE VOICE

Change the verb from the passive voice to the active voice in order to gain directness. (See EMPHASIS.)

Verbs that take a direct object are in the *active voice:*

The referee *blew* the whistle. (The word *whistle* is the direct object of *blew,* a verb in the *active* voice.)

When the direct object becomes the subject, the verb changes to a form of the verb "to be" plus a past participle and is said to be in the *passive voice:*

The whistle *was blown.* (The word "whistle" in the previous example was a direct object, but now it is the subject. The verb *was blown*—a form of "to be" plus a past participle—is in the *passive* voice.)

Weak passive voice: With the changing of seasons there comes a change in the type of clothing *to be worn.*

Direct active voice: **With the changing of seasons there comes a change in the type of clothing** *people wear.*

Passive: In the fall, cotton clothes *are stored away* by families and all that *can be seen* is bulky woolens.

Active: **In the fall,** *families store away* **their cotton clothes and all** *one can see* **is bulky woolens.**

Passive: I am sure this *can be done* by us if the money *can be found.*

Active: **I am sure** *we can do* **this if** *we can find* **the money.**

QUOTATION MARKS "   "

Use a pair of quotation marks (" ") 1. to enclose a passage of directly quoted words; 2. to draw attention to words applied in an unusual sense; and 3. to set off the titles of chapters, articles, stories, and poems published as *part* of a complete book or magazine.

When using other punctuation marks at the end of a quoted passage, always keep the period and comma *before* the end quotation mark. Always put semicolons and colons *after* the end quotation mark.

1. DIRECTLY QUOTED PASSAGES.

Examples:

The stewardess said, "Fasten your seat belts, please." Alexander Pope says that hope "springs eternal in the human breast."

Do not use quotation marks for indirect quotations:

Misuse: My brother said "that he was unhappy about the outcome."

Revision: Remove the quotation marks. **My brother said that he was unhappy about the outcome.** (Quotation marks would be used if this sentence were changed to a direct quotation, as follows: My brother said, "I am unhappy about the outcome.")

Quotations broken by "he said," "she said," etc.:

"I suppose," he remarked, "that success comes only with time."
(Since the quoted passage is one complete sentence, the interrupting words are set off by commas and *not* followed by a period or semicolon.)

"I understand the plan," Jim said. "I think it might work." (In this case, two separate sentences are quoted. *Jim said* must be followed by a period, for it marks the end of one quoted sentence.)

When quoting long prose passages, however, do not use quotation marks. Instead, indent the entire passage five spaces to the right (a few more spaces for the first line of a paragraph) and single-space if you are typing.

Example:

The author sums up in a nutshell the basic conditions that have shaped Spain's cultural development:

Spain is a world apart from the rest of Europe, separated by climatic differences and isolated in time as well as in space. Bounded by water on three sides, and on the fourth cut off by the barrier of the Pyrenees, she was for three hundred years, from the VIIIth to the XIth centuries, virtually under the domination of an oriental power—that of the Moors, whose culture was not only more advanced than that of any part of Europe, but also profoundly different from any European civilization.

—Enriqueta Harris
Spanish Painting

When quoting one or two lines of poetry, follow the examples for directly quoted passages.

Example:

Wallace Stevens is playing a musical joke when he writes, "Chieftain Iffucan of Azcan in caftan/ Of tan with henna hackles, halt!" (Note the slash used to show the line-end.)

When quoting more than two lines of poetry, do not use quotation marks. Simply indent the whole passage as for long prose quotations, single-space if typing, and reproduce the original as it stands.

2. EMPHASIS OF WORDS APPLIED IN AN UNUSUAL SENSE:

Examples:

In the printing trade, an engraved plate is called a "cut."

The jazz musician I met said he "dug" me and enjoyed spending the evening at my "pad."

NOTE: Do *not* use quotes to try to get acceptance for lazy, imprecise language of your own:

In spite of Jerry's "goofing off," he was generally regarded as a very "sharp" character.

3. STORIES, ARTICLES, AND OTHER PARTS OF A BOOK OR MAGAZINE.

Examples:

One of my favorite stories is Hemingway's "The Killers."

When you read *Sister Carrie,* pay careful attention to the first chapter, "The Magnet Attracting: A Waif Amid Forces." (Note that the title of the whole book is underlined, or italicized, whereas the chapter title is in quotation marks.)

QUOTATION MARKS WITH OTHER PUNCTUATION:

1. Periods and commas are placed *inside* closing quotation marks:

Shakespeare said, "Unquiet meals make ill digestions."

Francis Bacon remarked that "the monuments of wit survive the monuments of power," and I wholly agree with him.

2. Colons and semicolons are placed *outside* closing quotation marks:

We had arrived at "the moment of truth": the matador extended his sword for the finishing stroke.

I know that "to err is human"; yet fifteen errors in one ball game is too much to forgive.

3. Question marks and exclamation points remain inside closing quotation marks *only* if they are a part of

the quoted passage, as in the first two examples below. Otherwise, such marks remain outside the quotation marks, as in the last two examples:

I asked her, "Is dinner ready?"

He shouted, "Advance or I'll fire!"

Did I just hear you say, "Dinner is ready"?

Stop saying "yes"!

In direct quotations, avoid the extra comma or period after a closing quotation mark:

Avoid: "Well, well!", he said.
Better: (Remove comma.) **"Well, well!" he said.**

Avoid: He asked, "What's your name?".
Better: (Remove the period.) **He asked, "What's your name?"**

4. Use single marks (' ') to set off a quotation within a quotation:

"When Caesar said 'I came, I saw, I conquered,' " my history teacher declared, "little did he know that he had invented the telegram."

ref   REFERENCE OF PRONOUN

Make the pronoun you have used clearly refer to a previous noun.

Weak: When John spoke to Peter, he said he didn't think *he'd* be invited to the party. (Does the last *he* refer to John or Peter?)
Revision: **When John spoke to Peter, he said, "I don't think I** (or *you*) **will be invited to the party."** (The use of direct quotation often solves these reference problems.)

Weak: She felt as if she would burst into tears, *which* made it difficult for her to speak. (The pronoun *which* is often incorrectly used, as it is here, to refer to the whole preceding main clause rather than to a single noun.)

Revision: She felt as if she would burst into tears, a *sensation which* **made it difficult for her to speak.** (Place a noun before *which* that sums up the whole idea referred to. When this method seems too awkward, try recasting a part or the whole of the sentence: *Feeling* as if she would burst into tears, *she found it difficult to speak.*)

Weak: Daily she scrubbed the floors, mended his clothes, cooked him three hearty meals fit for a king, and spoke only of things that would please him. *This* proved her utter devotion to him. (The pronoun *this* is awkwardly made to refer to the whole preceding sentence.)

Revision (of the second sentence): Combine the pronoun *this* with a noun, or perhaps an adjective-noun group, which sums up the ideas of the whole previous sentence. **This** *ceaseless slavery* **proved her utter devotion to him. Better, recast the entire passage:** *Daily, she proved her utter devotion to him by scrubbing* the floors, *mending* his clothes, *cooking* him three hearty meals fit for a king, and *speaking* only of things that would please him.

Weak: How can one not be happy when he sees the leaves return in the spring and the difference *it* makes in everything about him? (The pronoun *it* awkwardly refers to the whole previous clause, "the leaves return in the spring.")

Revision: How can one not be happy when he sees *the return of the leaves* **in the spring and the difference it makes in everything about him?** (Now *it* clearly refers to the noun *return*.)

---

rep | **REPETITION**

Do not awkwardly repeat the same word or idea you have used before. (See also WORDINESS.) The more serious problem is the repetition of the same idea—whether in similar form or not—throughout the whole length of a composition. Such repetition suggests that the writer has little to say but feels pressured to fill up space. Only in commercial advertising and political propaganda is repetition an effective substitute for ordered, detailed development of an idea. (See PARAGRAPHING.)

Repetition: A cool breeze was *blowing,* and the brownish gold leaves were being *blown* about by the wind.

Revision: Change *blown* to *swept,* or find some other good synonym. Sometimes, as in this case, the sentence would be better if it were condensed: **The brownish gold leaves were being swept about by the cool breeze.** (There is no need to refer to the breeze again, even by the synonym *wind.*

Repetition: The air was too cold, *and* while I was asleep it chilled me, *and* when I awoke my bones felt stiff.

Revision: Eliminate one of the *and*'s: **The air was too cold. While I was asleep it chilled me, and when I awoke my bones felt stiff.**

Repetition: The steam could be seen rising from the radiator. *The steam* turned to frost on the windowpane.

Revision: Change the second *steam* to the pronoun *it.* **The steam could be seen rising from the radiator. It turned to frost on the windowpane.**

Better, condense: The steam rising from the radiator turned to frost on the windowpane.

Repetition: He *walked up and down* and kept pacing about the room.

Revision: Avoid repeating the same idea. He kept pacing about the room.

RO   RUN-ON SENTENCE

Be careful not to run one sentence into the next with no punctuation separating them. **End the first sentence with a period, and begin the next with a capital letter.** (Do not join two sentences with a comma, either. This error, sometimes called a run-on sentence, is more usually referred to as a *comma splice.* See COMMA SPLICE.)

Run-on: The Chinese are wonderful Ping-Pong players they really deserve their world-champion status.
Revision: The Chinese are wonderful Ping-Pong players. They really deserve their world-champion status.

Run-on: She put on her bathing cap then she plunged into the water.
Revision 1:   She put on her bathing cap. Then she plunged into the water. (Although a period is correct, a semicolon would probably be better between *cap* and *then.* Look up the use of semicolons before conjunctive adverbs like *then, however,* and *therefore* under COMMA SPLICE.)

Revision 2: She put on her bathing cap, then plunged into the water. (Use fewer words wherever convenient. By eliminating the second *she* and adding a comma after *cap,* we are left with a single, smooth sentence.)

semi

SEMICOLON ;

1. Use the semicolon to separate sentence elements equal in rank when they contain commas.

2. Use the semicolon to separate two main clauses when they are closely related in idea but are *not* connected with a coordinating conjunction (*and, but, for, or, nor*).

1. EQUAL SENTENCE ELEMENTS CONTAINING COMMAS.

I introduced him to Jack Kreel, the president; Will Baum, the vice-president; Herb Dunn, the treasurer; and Frank Newhouse, the secretary.

2. MAIN CLAUSES NOT CONNECTED BY A CONJUNCTION.

It is not so much the threatening weather that concerns me; it is the dilapidated condition of the ship. (The ideas are closely related.)

Also use the semicolon between main clauses connected by certain conjunctive adverbs, like *however* and *therefore* (see COMMA SPLICE):

I would like to attend the conference; however, I have a prior appointment which I am unable to cancel.

Do not use the semicolon between a main clause and a phrase or subordinate clause:

Avoid: I do not like to eat orange peels; although I admit that in marmalade they are quite good.
Better: Change the semicolon to a comma. I do not like to

eat orange peels, although I admit that in marmalade they are quite good.

Avoid: The fire spread through the town in a matter of minutes; lighting up the sky with a devilish glare.

Better: Change the semicolon to a comma. The fire spread through the town in a matter of minutes, lighting up the sky with a devilish glare.

SS SENTENCE STRUCTURE

You have made an error in the structure of your sentence. If no more specific directions are given for correcting it, read it over carefully, sounding it aloud if you can. You can often hear an error that you cannot see. If you still cannot locate the trouble, you would do best to **rewrite the sentence** entirely. (See AWKWARDNESS and UNITY OF SENTENCE PARTS.)

SHIFT IN POINT OF VIEW

If they are not logically necessary, avoid shifts in
1. person—from *I* or *one* to *you;* 2. subject and voice;
3. tense; 4. mood.

1. SHIFTS IN PERSON.

Shift: If one stops to watch them work, *you* are greeted with
a smile.
**Revised: If one stops to watch them work, *one* is greeted
with a smile.**

Shift: This was a morning that made me button up my jacket
and made *you* wish *you* had worn a topcoat.
**Revised: This was a morning that made me button up my
jacket and wish *I* had worn a topcoat.** (No need to repeat
"made me.")

2. SHIFTS IN SUBJECT AND VOICE.

Shift: *A party was attended by us* after we were graduated.
(Notice the awkward passive voice of the verb that makes
party the subject.)

Revised: *We attended a party* **after we were graduated.** (Now the subject of both clauses is the same, *we,* and both verbs are in the *active* voice. See PASSIVE VOICE.)

3. SHIFTS IN TENSE.

Shift: He rushed to catch his train but *misses* it by half a minute. (Needless shift from past to present tense.)
Revised: **He rushed to catch his train but** *missed* **it by half a minute.**

4. SHIFTS IN MOOD.

The usual shifts in mood likely to occur as an error in your writing are shifts from the *command* (imperative) form of the verb to the ordinary *indicative* form of the verb, as in the following example:

Shift: Be sure to visit the science exhibition, and then *you must go* to the art show.
Revised: **Be sure to visit the science exhibition, and then** *go* **to the art show.** (Both verbs, "be" and "go," are now in the command form.)

NOTE: In formal writing, *were* is preferred to *was* in "If" clauses. Example: If the country *were* truly rich, it could feed itself. (*Were* is the *subjunctive mood* of the verb *was.*)

sub SUBORDINATION

When ideas are *not* of equal importance, do not arrange them in a series of short, choppy sentences or in a series of main clauses connected by *and*'s, *but*'s, and *so*'s.

Give emphasis to the more important ideas by keeping them as main clauses. Change lesser ideas into subordinate clauses, phrases, and even single words where possible.

Examples:

Poor: Her employer did not care for her, *so* he refused to write her a letter of recommendation. (Two equally emphatic main clauses.)

Better: *Because* **her employer did not care for her, he refused to write her a letter of recommendation.** (The first main clause, less emphatic than the second, is changed into a subordinate clause beginning with *because*.)

Poor: He was exhausted. He had been swimming too long and was doubled up by a sudden cramp. He called for help. (This is an awkward series of choppy sentences.)

Better: **Exhausted from swimming too long and doubled up by a sudden cramp, he called for help.** (The first two sentences are turned into phrases.)

Poor: The moon was glowing and it looked like the face of a snowman.

Better: **The** *glowing* **moon looked like the face of a snowman.** (The first main clause is condensed into the single word *glowing*.)

T   TENSE

1. One of the verbs of your sentence may not be in the correct time relation with the other(s). Check to see whether you are using the proper sequence of tenses.

2. Use your dictionary to find the correct forms of "irregular" verbs (for example, *choose, chose, chosen*).

3. Do not shift tenses without good reason. (See *Shifts in Tense* under SHIFT IN POINT OF VIEW.)

4. Use the present tense for plot summaries.

1. SEQUENCE OF TENSES.

If the time when an action takes place is the *same* in both the main clause and the subordinate clause, then the tense of both verbs must be the same.

Examples:

When he *arrived*, the crowd *greeted* him with a long ovation.

As he slowly *turns*, he *balances* himself with his arms.

If the action in the subordinate clause is earlier than that in the main clause, put the subordinate verb in the appropriate past tense.

Examples:

I am informed that he *has worked* wonders. (Main verb, *am,* is in present tense; subordinate verb, *has worked,* is in present perfect tense. The present perfect expresses a time earlier than the present.)

I was informed that he *had worked* wonders. (The past perfect, *had worked,* expresses a time prior to some understood time in the past. This "understood" past time is expressed by the simple past tense, *was.*)

When you are expressing *a permanent fact,* however, the present tense is used:

I was informed that penicillin *works* wonders. (Use *works,* not *worked.*)

Keep an infinitive in the present tense if it expresses the same time as the action of the main verb; keep it in the past tense if it expresses a time before the action of the main verb.

Examples:

I would have liked *to go* with you.

I would like *to go* with you. (In both these cases, although the main verb differs in tense, the present infinitive concerns "going" at the same time that the "liking," or desire to go, is expressed.)

I would like *to have gone* with you. (Here the past infinitive is used because the wish in the present concerns an action already completed in the past.)

Overkill: I would *have liked* to *have gone* with you. (Do not use the past infinitive together with the past tense of the main verb. Use one or the other, as shown in the examples above, but not both at the same time.)

2. IRREGULAR VERBS.

Most English verbs are "regular," forming their past tense and past participle in *-ed:* I *waited,* I have *waited.*

Once you know the present tense, *wait,* you know all the other tenses. There is a troublesome group of "irregular" verbs, however, whose present tense (I *break*) is no clue to the past tense (I *broke*) or to the compound past tenses formed with the past participle (I have *broken: broken* is the past participle).

If you are in doubt about the past tense forms of a verb, look up the verb in the dictionary under its present tense form (*bite,* for example) and you will find the past tense (*bit*) and past participle (*bitten*) listed in order right after it. Below is a list of some of the most frequently misused irregular verbs:

PRESENT	PAST	PAST PARTICIPLE
I *blow*	I *blew*	I have *blown*
I *bring*	I *brought*	I have *brought*
I *burst*	I *burst*	I have *burst*
I *do*	I *did*	I have *done*
I *drink*	I *drank*	I have *drunk*
I *drive*	I *drove*	I have *driven*
I *eat*	I *ate*	I have *eaten*
I *forbid*	I *forbade*	I have *forbidden*
I *go*	I *went*	I have *gone*
I *lay* (bricks)	I *laid* (bricks)	I have *laid* (bricks)
I *lie* (down)	I *lay* (down)	I have *lain* (down)
I *ring*	I *rang*	I have *rung*
I *rise*	I *rose*	I have *risen*
I *run*	I *ran*	I have *run*
I *seek*	I *sought*	I have *sought*
I *sing*	I *sang*	I have *sung*
I *steal*	I *stole*	I have *stolen*
I *swim*	I *swam*	I have *swum*
I *swing*	I *swung*	I have *swung*
I *write*	I *wrote*	I have *written*

3. TENSE SHIFTS.

Changes in tense must occur for a good reason. In the following example, there is no justification for the shift:

Shift: I ran to his house and tried to find him, but I *arrive* too late.

Revised: Change *arrive* to *arrived.* I ran to his house and tried to find him, but I *arrived* too late. (If in the above sentence it seems natural to you to use *arrive* rather than *arrived,* the problem may be that in your daily conversational habits you are not used to using, or even hearing, the past tense endings of verbs in standard English. If this is your problem, ask your instructor to recommend materials that will help you practise the standard tense forms.

NOTE: Do not drop the tense-endings from past participles used as adjectives:

The church boasted ornate, *stain* glass windows. (Change *stain* to *stained.*)

4. PLOT SUMMARIES.

Use the present tense in summarizing the plot of a short story, novel, play, or film.

Examples:

In a disheveled state, trying to appear insane, Hamlet *visits* Ophelia and *hints* that the cause of his sorry appearance *is* to some extent her recent conduct.

---

trans   # TRANSITIONS

Add a word or phrase to form a logical bridge, or *transition,* **between the two thoughts.** Without such a connecting element, the second thought does not follow smoothly or logically from the first. (See also COHERENCE.)

Examples:

Transition missing: I liked him. I thought his table manners needed improving. (The sudden contrast between these two thoughts is not smoothly bridged over.)
Better: I liked him. *However,* **I thought his table manners needed improving.**

Transition missing: On the whole, I think that educated men have made the best politicians. There are exceptions. (The second sentence follows too abruptly.)

Better: On the whole, I think that educated men have made the best politicians. *Of course,* **there are exceptions.**

Note the use of transitional words and phrases (italicized) in the following—somewhat shortened—paragraph by Schopenhauer:

> What the address is to a letter, the title should be to a book; *in other words,* its main object should be to bring the book to those amongst the public who will take an interest in its contents. It should, *therefore,* be expressive. . . . The worst titles of all are those which have been stolen, *those, I mean,* which have already been borne by other books; for they are *in the first place* a plagiarism, and *secondly* the most convincing proof of a total lack of originality in the author. . . .

tr

TRANSPOSE

Change the order of the indicated letters or words to gain a clearer or more idiomatic reading. (See MIS-PLACED MODIFIERS.) The proofreader's symbol ⌒ is often used to point out which elements are to be *transposed* (reversed).

Examples:

Incorrect order of letters: He tride hard.
Corrected: He tried hard.

Poor word order: I *only* hear good things about him. (*Only* is misplaced.)

Poor word order: Government and industry must, *if we are to keep nature's balance from being irrevocably destroyed,* cooperate.
Better: If we are to keep nature's balance from being irrevocably destroyed, government and industry must cooperate.

TRITENESS

Avoid writing that is dull, commonplace, and uninteresting in either thought or expression. (See the section on CLICHÉS, which are a special case of trite language.)

Example of a trite paragraph:

Skyjacking is a crime against humanity and should be outlawed throughout the world. The victims are always innocent people, including men, women, and children, and the airlines, too, almost always lose a lot of money. Their insurance rates probably go up as well. Skyjacking is a terrible disease that ought to be stamped out. Worst of all is the added insecurity everyone now feels when boarding an airplane. It is bad enough to have to worry about a crash due to mechanical failure, but now one has to worry about being blown to bits in flight by a maniac with a hand grenade. The maniacs think they are in the right, but the rest of the world ought to get together and start the ball rolling to prevent these lunatics from reaching their goals.

Comment:

The writer of this paragraph has nothing more to say than the boringly obvious. He is either too tired to think, or else he supposes that English teachers want to see writing-for-writing's-sake. If he were to discuss skyjacking with his friends, would he ever dare bore them with trivial notions like these? (Trite ideas are usually couched in trite language. Note the *clichés* like "crime against humanity" and "start the ball rolling." Note the repetition of the same idea, never *developed,* in the first, fourth, and seventh sentences. See also PARAGRAPHING and REPETITION.)

UNITY OF SENTENCE PARTS

Keep your sentences free of unrelated ideas and distracting details. All the parts of a sentence must contribute clearly and significantly to one main idea.

Non-unified: The gravest danger to the drought-stricken area is now disease, but there is no relief effort that functions effectively without a central organizing agency. (Beginning with "but," the second half of the sentence *distracts* from the idea of the first half. The ideas are not closely enough related and therefore compete for attention.)

Unified: The gravest danger to the drought-stricken area is now disease. *Nations all over the world are sending medical teams and supplies,* but there is no relief effort that functions effectively without a central organizing agency. (The two ideas of the original sentence are best expressed in separate sentences. The ideas were too distantly related, and what was missing was a logical bridge connecting them. Such a bridge is now supplied in the passage in italics. See also COHERENCE.)

Distracting detail: Sometimes those who wish to save our environment, in their fight for clean skies, earth, and water, so that the required oxygen level of the atmosphere will be maintained by fostering the growth of vegetation and plankton, have to oppose government agencies consisting of so-called experts in ecology and regional planning (frequently no more expert than you or I) who are unduly influenced by private pressure groups.

Improved: Sometimes those who wish to save our environment have to oppose so-called experts in government agencies who are unduly influenced by private pressure groups. (Any details worth saving can be brought into the composition at some other point. Do not clutter your sentence with distracting details simply because they occur to you at the moment of writing.)

VARIETY IN SENTENCE PATTERNS

To avoid a "choppy" style, **use a variety of sentence types.** For interesting sentence sequences, alternate *simple* with *compound, complex,* and *compound-complex* sentences. If you employ this easy technique, your style—and your grade, too—will improve considerably.

SIMPLE SENTENCE. A simple sentence contains only one main clause. (The sentence you have just read is a simple sentence.) A series of simple sentences in a row can result in choppiness.

Example:

I enjoy going to the movies. I like watching murder mysteries best. I sit at the edge of my seat at the high points of such pictures. (None of these sentences is individually bad. But together they are monotonous. Each sentence begins unoriginally in the same way: the pattern is constantly *subject,* then *verb.* See SUBORDINATION after you learn the other sentence types below.)

COMPOUND SENTENCE. A compound sentence consists of two or more simple sentences, or main clauses, usually connected by a coordinating conjunction, like *and, but, or, nor,* or *for.*

Example:

Mary still works as a secretary, *but* Harriet has already become a dress designer.

COMPLEX SENTENCE. A complex sentence contains one main clause and one or more subordinate clauses.

Example:

Although I sat at the edge of my seat, I did not forget that it was only a movie, after all. (There are two subordinate clauses in this sentence, one beginning with *although,* the other with *that.*)

COMPOUND-COMPLEX SENTENCE. A compound-complex sentence contains at least *two* main clauses and at least *one* subordinate clause.

Example:

When we are studying, we should not let outside influences distract us, for our school work deserves our utmost concentration. (The sentence contains one subordinate clause, beginning with *when,* and two main clauses, one beginning with *we* and the other with *for.*)

Express your ideas in fewer words. Do not "puff out" your sentences with unnecessary, repetitious phrasing.

Examples:

Wordy: In my opinion, I personally feel that our system of government is best. ("In my opinion," "personally," and "I feel" are three ways of saying about the same thing. Don't use them all at once!)

Better: I feel that our system of government is best.

Wordy: In the modern world of today, mankind is enjoying the fruits of a long technological revolution which took place throughout the entire period of the machine age.

Better: **Today mankind is enjoying the fruits of a long technological revolution.** (All that has been left out is mere repetition and adds nothing. See REPETITION.)

PROGRESS CHART

You will find the columns below useful for recording the errors you have made in your written assignments throughout the term. Use the first column to list the errors in your first composition, the second column for the errors in your second assignment, etc. For convenience, use the correction symbols only, and next to each write how many times that particular error occurs in that composition: for example, FRAG (2). Record major errors first, then minor. Hopefully, you should see your progress—and your main problems—revealed more and more as the term goes on.

English ———.

ASGT. # DATE GRADE	ASGT. # DATE GRADE	ASGT. # DATE GRADE	ASGT. # DATE GRADE	ASGT. # DATE GRADE	ASGT. # DATE GRADE

SPELLING PROGRESS CHART

List in the columns below the *correct* forms for the words you misspell on each composition. Your chart will develop into an excellent diagnosis of your spelling problem.

English ———.

ASGT. # DATE GRADE	ASGT. # DATE GRADE	ASGT. # DATE GRADE	ASGT. # DATE GRADE	ASGT. # DATE GRADE	ASGT. # DATE GRADE

SPELLING PROGRESS CHART

List in the columns below the *correct* forms for the words you misspell on each composition. Your chart will develop into an excellent diagnosis of your spelling problem.

English _____.

ASGT. # DATE GRADE	ASGT. # DATE GRADE	ASGT. # DATE GRADE	ASGT. # DATE GRADE	ASGT. # DATE GRADE	ASGT. # DATE GRADE	ASGT. # DATE GRADE

SPELLING PROGRESS CHART

List in the columns below the *correct* forms for the words you misspell on each composition. Your chart will develop into an excellent diagnosis of your spelling problem.

English ———

ASGT. # DATE GRADE	ASGT. # DATE GRADE	ASGT. # DATE GRADE	ASGT. # DATE GRADE	ASGT. # DATE GRADE	ASGT. # DATE GRADE

SPELLING PROGRESS CHART

List in the columns below the *correct* forms for the words you misspell on each composition. Your chart will develop into an excellent diagnosis of your spelling problem.

English ———.

ASGT. # DATE GRADE	ASGT. # DATE GRADE	ASGT. # DATE GRADE	ASGT. # DATE GRADE	ASGT. # DATE GRADE	ASGT. # DATE GRADE

PROGRESS CHART

You will find the columns below useful for recording the errors you have made in your written assignments throughout the term. Use the first column to list the errors in your first composition, the second column for the errors in your second assignment, etc. For convenience, use the correction symbols only, and next to each write how many times that particular error occurs in that composition: for example, FRAG (2). Record major errors first, then minor. Hopefully, you should see your progress—and your main problems—revealed more and more as the term goes on.

English ——————.

ASGT. # DATE GRADE	ASGT. # DATE GRADE	ASGT. # DATE GRADE	ASGT. # DATE GRADE	ASGT. # DATE GRADE	ASGT. # DATE GRADE

PROGRESS CHART

You will find the columns below useful for recording the errors you have made in your written assignments throughout the term. Use the first column to list the errors in your first composition, the second column for the errors in your second assignment, etc. For convenience, use the correction symbols only, and next to each write how many times that particular error occurs in that composition: for example, FRAG (2). Record major errors first, then minor. Hopefully, you should see your progress—and your main problems—revealed more and more as the term goes on.

English ———.

ASGT. # DATE GRADE	ASGT. # DATE GRADE	ASGT. # DATE GRADE	ASGT. # DATE GRADE	ASGT. # DATE GRADE	ASGT. # DATE GRADE